THE
JOURNEY
TO RECOVERY

To Madelene

With love

S. L Shane

x x

(Author)

THE
JOURNEY
TO RECOVERY

A STORY OF HOPE, COURAGE, DETERMINATION AND SURVIVAL

EMILY COLLINS

authorHOUSE®

AuthorHouse™
1663 Liberty Drive
Bloomington, IN 47403
www.authorhouse.com
Phone: 1-800-839-8640

First published by AuthorHouse   10/18/2011

ISBN: 978-1-4670-0947-8 (sc)
ISBN: 978-1-4670-0948-5 (ebk)

Printed in the United States of America

CONTENTS

This is my own personal journey with such a magical outcome. So when you read this, don't feel sympathy for that never helped me. But all I ask is that you can learn from my experience and help this to make you a much stronger, wiser person.

This is why I sit here today telling you my journey so that this may bring those of you who feel helpless just a little bit of hope. If I can do that, to even just one person it will make my entire journey worthwhile.

I come from a large family. In fact one of eight children. I was born in 1986. I have one younger brother, and one younger sister all the rest are older than me. I grew up in a small village.

My parents divorced when I was aged 15. I don't know exactly why they divorced I just presume they no longer had the love there that there was at the start of the marriage.

My childhood up until about the age of 12 was what I would call an average childhood. The usual brothers and sisters arguing and fighting and calling each other all the names under the sun one minute, then laughing and playing together the next.

In primary school I was above average in my English but average in all my other subjects. I had many friends in my primary school and never fell short of a laugh. By the time I reached secondary school. Things were very different.

Things at home didn't seem quite right but I was never sure why. So I learnt to adjust to this new atmosphere.

I realized my mother had ways of coping that were not helpful. My mother's ways of handling things were so out of control she didn't see her children around her who were craving her love. She either could not see this or the things she used to cope with her life was just so intense she was unable to resist this. Even for her children's sake.

After realizing that day in school what caused this atmosphere at home was just the start of a much more intense atmosphere. And god, if I knew now that from this day just how much my life was about to change I would sometimes turn the clock back.

Most people at 12 years old was planning what they want to do with there dream future. I was no different. Except my future went far off the scale to the one I had once dreamed.

I remember walking many miles of the countryside looking at the beautiful views in the distance with the sun going down in the distance just behind the hills. It was an amazing view. I used to get a great feeling of peace. It was just the scene that calmed my whole life down. I could take myself away from all my worries and just let them go. At least for a little while. Then I came back to reality.

CHAPTER ONE

When I was 9 and wanted to go out to play with my friends I was told by a medium I had a gift and that I could also develop this gift and become a medium later in life.

This all came about after we had some strange going on's in our family home and I had seen a spirit.

The going on's at home became more dangerous by day until we realized our home was haunted and needed to be exercised by a medium. It was when this took place I was told about this gift I had.

To me that wasn't anything I was just more interested in when I was next going to meet up with my friends.

Due to our house being haunted and me seeing the spirit it somehow reached the local and main newspapers and even the headlines of the BBC and ITV news. How this came about I am not entirely sure. I was too young to understand but I was defiantly not too young to remember the confufle of the interviews and the consequences of being on the news or in the papers.

This at first made me popular to some but a bullying target for others.

CHAPTER TWO

My heart was pounding as I walked into the kitchen and saw my mother staggering over the cooker trying to cook the evening tea. I stood there and took a deep breath before blurting out.

"mum, you're going to die" how was I meant to know any different when I had just been told in school that if you drink too much it can affect your liver and cause a slow painful death. All I could see was a picture in my head of this being my mum.

At this point my mother turned to me. I could see the red anger in her eyes, her face turning from red to purple with every second that passed. Suddenly she raged what do you mean? I trembled in answer. The drink it will kill you. Another roar came from my mum apart from this one was closer and louder. "Don't you tell me what to do" in defense and fear I whispered "I just don't want you to die mum, I love you."

Just as my tears started rolling and I was in need of my mothers arms around me telling me it was all o.k. I got a blow from my mothers hand to my head. I could feel each blow after blow of my mother's hand bouncing of my head. I turned to try and run but as I speeded through the back door my foot misplaced one of the steps and I fell to the ground. By this time 4 of my older sisters had come to see what all the noise was about.

I wished they could have protected me, told my mum to stop, but instead as I was on the floor trying to get back on my feet with such a struggle due to the fear running through my legs that was making them shake so bad I couldn't stabilize. My sisters pinned me to the floor and each sister pinned down a limb each.

I was so scared I was horrified as tears streamed down my face and I tried to plead with my eyes my mother gripped her hands around my neck. As I felt her grip get tighter and tighter I knew I was becoming closer and closer to death. In my mind I feared death and knew I had to say my last words before I died. I repeated again I love you all and I am so sorry, please remember I love you.

Suddenly my flight or fight response kicked in. I gained energy at the time I thought I lacked it. I managed to get one of my sisters to loosen their grip and I swung my arm across until it hit my mother in the face.

Mum released her grip as much as that was comforting as I managed to gasp for air. I knew it would make my mother angrier. As soon as I had enough oxygen I screamed someone call the police. I wasn't sure if anyone would have heard me and even if they had heard me if they would have acted upon my plea for help. With this is mind I ran back into the house in a daze hearing my mothers words in the distance yelling "get back in that house".

As I got into the house I ran straight towards the telephone to dial 999. My mother watched me make this move and grabbed the receiver out of my shaking hand and hit me across the head with it.

Yelling don't you dare do that. With this I was pushed out into the hallway. I was punched and kicked at again and again.

My younger brother and sister then aged 1 and 2 unfortunately had to witness this. My youngest brother shouted down "mummy please don't kill Emily" with this I told my mother she could hit me but don't let the kids witness it and to take me into the lounge if she wanted to continue. I then pushed and dragged myself into the lounge so they didn't have to witness this horrifying experience.

Mum continued to blow a few more punches until my older sisters voice said "mum, stop the police are here.' That first breath I took after that was of relief. My mother didn't forget to get the biggest and final blow to my head in though.

The police came in, mum was yelling take her away. A police officer went into the lounge with my mother whilst another came into the kitchen with me. They asked me what had gone on and I just froze in all the shock of what had just happened to me. They asked if I knew I was bleeding from my ears and nose. I just said "I don't know where I'm bleeding from; I'm in so much pain."

The police told me to pack some clothes and I was to go with them for the night. I begged that I done nothing wrong and wanted to stay home. But the police told me I was just going away to let things blow over at home. I done as I was asked and I followed the police down the path. I turned around to face towards the house unaware of where the police were going to take me.

As I looked back my mother was stood at the front door telling the police "take her away I don't love her anyway"

The police took me to the local police station. They asked where my father was. I knew he was at work but couldn't bring myself to tell the police incase dad didn't understand.

As the paperwork was done and the police made me take all my clothes off in front of them so they could write down all my cuts and bruises. Whilst all this was taking place somehow they managed to contact my father who had just turned up at the police station. The police asked if I would like to see my dad. I said yes.

My father walked into the room he just burst into tears and said "who done this to you" I told him it was my mother and sisters and he asked why I had never told him. He was asked to go home and pick me up some clothes as I hadn't taken enough. He then went to do this and as he was collecting more belongings the police explained I was going away in care on a police protection order to give things time to calm down.

As this was completed and my father returned, the police asked me to get into the police vehicle so they could take me to different police station so that social services could pick me up from there. As I got into the vehicle and tears welled up into my eyes I finally broke as I turned to look back at my father who was breaking his heart out begging the police not to take me. He got so distraught he fell to his knees. As tears streamed down my face and my heart tore with pain and confusion I was taken away.

A little while later social services had collected me and took me to a foster placement. I refused to speak and withdrew and all that came out my mouth is 'I'm going home tomorrow but for now I just want to go to bed.'

As my foster mother showed me the bedroom I was to sleep in. I just sat on the edge of the bed and cried and cried until I could cry no more. I returned home on my own will after 72 hours which was when the police protection order ceased and I demanded to go home where I thought was meant to be, a place where I belonged but too soon did I realize how wrong this thinking was.

CHAPTER THREE

When I returned home things went really well for a few days. I felt like all this could become the past and forgotten and go back to a normal family life [not that I had ever experienced this] and how wrong was I?

It was my first evening home my mother had not been drinking [she tended to manage to control her drink habits at the right times so that I looked a liar and she could play the perfect mum and explain to others how much of a problem child she had so that people would feed my mother on sympathy. But what made me so angry was they were not just feeding her sympathy but also her denial and giving her the excuse to get another drink down her throat].

Anyway this evening my mother was laid in her bed watching TV when I went upstairs to give her a kiss goodnight. As I lent towards her to give her a kiss she grabbed my hand and said she was sorry and how she would treat me so different from then on and that she did love me. I said it was ok but asked her why. She asked me to sit on her bed as she said that when she was pregnant with me she wanted an abortion but my father got her to keep me. When I was nearly due she hadn't felt me move for a few days so my father made her go for an antenatal check up. It was then the doctor explained my food tube was not connected and that I may not survive but they needed to get her down for emergency cesarean. When I was born I was whisked away my mother explained she had told herself I was dead so when the doctor came in with me in his hands crying she couldn't believe it she had prepared herself to be told I had died. The doctor handed me over to mum and said to my mother and father you are two very lucky people she has made it but is still very weak. [So this was my mother's reason for nearly killing her own daughter]

After a few days mum was back drinking, a few thumps were thrown around and I had enough and ran away.

I ran to a friend's house and we stayed at her uncles who I had never met. At the time I didn't care as long as I never had to go back home.

As we entered her uncles 2 bedroom flat I could see he had been drinking wine and the evidence was on the table in front of him. Anxiety rose straight away knowing there was drink around and what this could mean.

As Ian welcomed us with a hello and offered us a drink. I refused the offer. My mate took the offer up as she explained why I had run away from home and needed somewhere safe to stay for the night.

My friend and I went to sit on a 3 seated settee we sat at opposite ends so the middle seat was free. Ian at first was sat in one of the single chairs. Then as my friend and Ian had a few more drinks and started to get drunk, Ian moved onto the settee in between us both.

He put his arm around my shoulder. I shuffled a bit to try and say I was uncomfortable. But whether Ian decided to ignore this or didn't realize I don't know. Whatever way he kept his arm around my shoulders then slowly lowered his hands down my chest until he was touching my breasts over my clothes. He continued to lower his hands down my body and over my stomach until he was touching my vagina over my clothes. Tears started rolling down my face. I felt confused. I kept trying to tell myself that he might not realize where he's hands were touching me and that he didn't mean anything by it. But as I continued to try and convince myself of this, Outside what was going on in my mind and as I brought myself back to reality I could see he had moved his hands back up onto my breasts and was now touching my breasts under my clothes.

I felt disgusted his dirty hands all over my body. Something was stopping my speech. It could have been fear all I know was as much as I was trying, no words would come out of my mouth.

By this time Ian's hands had worked themselves down to my vagina under my clothes. I knew I had to stop this but how? I was just 12 years old; he was a big strong very drunk man.

I felt dirty and disgusting and managed to blurt out to my friend in-between my silent sobs 'can we go to bed now I'm tired' my friend responded and said yes.

As we got up and made our way into Ian's spare room. I opened the door to a room painted black with black curtains, a single bed and a double bed. I knew my friend would want the light of. But I didn't want to stay in a pitch black room with all my scary thoughts. Not without someone to protect me.

I so much wished my mum would hold me tell me all that happened was a bad dream and that I was safe and could go to sleep thinking of the beautiful sea with an amazing sunset. But this was never going to happen especially not here and it wouldn't have even happened if I was at home having a bad dream.

I lay down in the single bed as my friend pushed the door too so that it was left slightly open and she jumped into the double bed. I lay in my bed eyes transfixed to the door in fear, and my tears just would not stop.

As all what had happened was swirling around in my head I could see the bedroom door slowly opening and a shadow come through the door and push it too. Ian was in the bedroom somewhere it was too dark to see where but I could hear his footsteps walking around the room and I lay praying he that he doesn't come near me.

I felt his hands creep under my cover I tried to hold it tight so he wouldn't be able to touch me but my strength wasn't enough. He started to touch my breasts and vagina which must have only been for a few minutes but at that time it felt like hours. Then he stood up again I couldn't see where he was heading I knew he was still in the room but I didn't know where.

I laid in fear as tears streamed down my face. I started to hear orgasms and I knew it wasn't me. There was only one other person it could be. My friend. I had to stop this I had to protect my friend. I tried to rationalize in my head what I could say or do to stop this. There was no rational thinking in my head apart from the longer I spent thinking the further my friend would be hurt.

I crept to the bottom of my bed I went over to the light switch. I stayed facing the light as I switched it on for fear that what was thinking might just be true. As the light switched on I said the first thing that came to my head. 'Right I'm going now'. I heard Ian say oh shit. As I turned I caught Ian pulling up his pants and trousers. He walked over to me and asked me to go into the lounge. I tried to say no as I was scared of what his plan to do with me was. But he kept asking me to go in he just wanted a chat with me.

He followed me into the lounge as I sat myself in the single chair in silence. After a few minutes of uncomfortable silence Ian said to me 'if you're going to shout at me then shout'.

I told him I didn't want to shout at him I just wanted to check that my friend was ok. He said go on then.

I went back into the bedroom where my friend was sat on the edge of her bed. She asked me what was wrong as she saw my tear stained face. I said 'do you know what just happened' as she nodded she said are you ok what's happened to you.

As I sat and explained to her in detail the events of the evening she could sense how shaken up I was. I got up and said I'm not staying here I'm going home. I was in my nightclothes and my friend said you can't go home yet not only are you in your pajamas and it's a long way but it's late at night. I don't care I screeched back at her. She told me to go outside with her and have a cigarette to calm down. Then we could sleep things off and go home the next morning as soon as daylight hits. With this agreement I went back inside with her but I had not intentions of sleeping I was too scared and shaken up.

The following morning we went into the lounge and my friend told Ian we were going home. He said he wanted to give us a lift and my friend took him up on his offer. He asked me to sit in the front of his car but I declined so my friend ended up sitting in the front.

The journey home was silent until Ian parked outside my home and he said 'are you going to tell anyone' I said I didn't know but I probably wouldn't.

A few days had passed my behavior at school deteriated and I couldn't stop cleaning myself after my abuse. My eldest sister guessed what was wrong and told me to tell my mother. I told my mother about Ian and she called the police. I done a video statement and my friend came forward and done one too.

During this time a lot of things were going on at home. The beatings from my mother continued she had also started to torture me mentally after my abuse convincing me it was my entire fault and I deserved it. After being convinced I dropped the charges and so did my friend as she felt unable to take the case on, on her own. The police tried to persuade me to take it on and guaranteed me Ian would be sent to prison. But I still couldn't do it so all the police could do was keep the case open for 10 years incase I changed my mind.

CHAPTER FOUR

Meanwhile at home my beating continued and I was going in and out of care. [I kept returning home on my own will in hope that things would be different but they never were, until eventually I was put on a full care order.]

I was still only 12. I felt so unloved and like I wasn't wanted. I felt I didn't belong to society I was shifted from care home to care home like I was nobody. I started to self harm. Everyone hated me and I hated myself. I just wanted to die. I done several overdoses and cut myself every day. I found a release in it. Not only did I feel I deserved it but it gave me my only sense that I was real and that I was alive. It was like the blood that was dripping from my arms was all my emotions and feelings. It was easier and much less painful then shedding tears. My tears felt so painful and they came from the pit of my stomach.

I later explained my self harm like smoking or taking drugs. It was a release to my stress or emotions but later became an addiction. It was just like having a cigarette. If you try and give up cigarettes the urge becomes unbearable. Then when you have one there's that big sense of release. But then you regret what you have done and think that's it ive messed up I might aswel have another. This became just like my self harm.

I remember in one of my children's homes I was arrested for arson. I tried to kill myself by setting the children's home alight with me in it. The fire brigades came to put the fire out and the police arrested me for arson. But once I was questioned and explained I didn't mean to hurt anyone and I only wanted to kill myself. I was lucky and given a caution.

CHAPTER FIVE

After this placement I was 14 years old and went to live with a foster family John and Jayne. They were very nice foster parents and treated me well at the start.

I had settled in well and became close to both my foster parents and there birth son Ben. Ben wasn't at home all the time he worked in London during the week and came home for the weekends.

There was another foster girl in the placement called Claire with whom I became close to as well.

John and Jayne had taken us for the weekend to black pool so we could see black pool tower and experiment the rides at pleasure beach. I and Claire were sharing a room in the hotel and John and Jayne had a separate room.

When we went to the rides John kept repeatedly paying for me to go on the one I most enjoyed but wouldn't let Claire go on extra rides. I couldn't understand this at the time. Even though ive made sense of it now as it was a piece to the puzzle of what was next in store.

On several occasions on our trip away when I was getting dressed and undressed, I noticed John kept opening the door when I was half naked but each time he apologized and said he didn't realize I was getting changed. I found this a coincidence but I took his word for it. These things can happen. Yet was I to learn this was another piece of the puzzle I was about to encounter.

Within several days of arriving home things were going well. I was waiting for a placement at a local school place for children with behavioral problems. [You may wonder why I needed this but this will be explained as I continue my journey]. John had stayed close to me and on several occasions he tried to make a move on me with kissing him but I had avoided this and told him no.

This only happened when I was left alone with him which caused me to feel anxious each time I was left alone with him and I tried to always make a quick exit.

John had been doing work in the attic to convert the attic space into a bedroom so that they could get another foster child in.

It was on one of the mornings Jayne had decided to go shopping and leave me with John. As much as I tried to persuade her to let me go she refused and wanted to go alone as she wouldn't be long. The more I continued to try and persuade her, the more suspicious she became until she blurted out what's wrong with you staying here and that John was upstairs. I remained silent. THAT was the problem staying alone with John. Jayne left to go shopping.

After a few minutes the phone rang I called up to John to ask if he wanted me to answer he shouted back I would be grateful if you could.

I answered the phone I recall it being social services and that they gave me some good news regarding my schooling but I cant recall that exact news all I remember is saying I have to let John know I was exited and ran upstairs to the attic to tell him the good news.

As I told him John turned to sit on the ledge of the stairs and asked me to repeat what I said slowly. I sat down the opposite side on the ledge of the stairs and repeated the phone call from social services.

John rose and came towards me with open arms saying that's really good news isn't it. I stood and allowed John to hug me as we had been waiting along time for this news and it had been a long drawn out road.

As I allowed John to hug me I was pushed to the floor. My body was in shock and I just froze my sight had gone black. I was unable to see or unable to shout or scream due to the shock my body was in but I too sure was ABLE to feel something or someone penetrating me and hear Johns deep breath in my ear.

When this petrifying experience was over and Johns released me from his grip, I went downstairs to the toilet. I saw blood in my underwear and this confirmed my worst fear. That something did penetrate me and I was possibly raped.

My mind was all mixed up. I started crying. How could I not be sure of what happened?, Did I want this?, Am I dirty?, Why didn't I scream or hit him off?, I feel so dirty did I ask for this?, Was it my fault?. [These questions remained in me for years and built up a lot of anger inside me;]

I hated myself, my self esteem. Well what was it. I deserved to hurt myself. Two people had taken advantage sexually, my mother physically. There must be something about me I must ask for it. I need punishing I'm a bad person].

As all this rolled through my mind and tears stained my face. I returned upstairs in the attic to John. I wanted answers I wanted to know what had just happened.

As I went into the attic and climbed the stairs I asked John if he wanted a cup of tea. He took me up the offer.

As I returned to the attic with the tea John asked me if I was ok. [What did he truly think?] I said "no, what happened?" John told me to put it to the back of my mind. Then I repeated "no what happened?" he told me it was sex without the ruff bits. This just confused me more [and still does] so I left it there.

I heard Jayne come home from shopping and I went downstairs to see her. I so much wish she could mind read it was too hard for me to tell her about John. I mean that's his wife. To them I was just a messed up child who needed a home. And I thought that Jayne might look at it as jealousy that there family was so close and loved one another. And me and my family didn't seem to know what that was. So I was out to destroy.

Jayne sensed something was wrong and kept asking if I was o.k. my very well practiced yes of course I am kept slipping out when I just wish I could tell someone and I could be reassured I was o.k. and that I was safe.

My mothers and my relationship was lets just say a little bit strained, but no matter what happened between us I still wished especially at times like this my mums warm arms would wrap around me like the wings off angels. And protect me and let me know I'm safe. A daughter always needs her mother no matter what. But not once, not once in my times of distress could I have this that most people take for granted. No matter how much I needed it or longed for it. In my world this never happened. It would be just like something I would see on television. My life was crumbling around me. Life for me was no life.

I went upstairs to pack my belongings. It was the same day this incident took place and Ben returned home from London for the weekend. He came to say hello and saw I had been crying and was packing my bags, "where you going?' what's gone on?" again my typical "nothing" come out. "So why are you packing?" Ben asked. I started fluttering around and Ben demanded me to sit down and talk. I just blurted out "it's your dad" "what" he yelched. I thought he was angry and that I had said too much already.

Ben started shaking his head and under his breath was saying "no, no" he looked up at me and said "is it what I'm thinking" as fear struck my eyes and my tears ran down my swollen face I nodded my head. "Oh no, not again!" Ben screeched as he rose to his feet and ran down the stairs.

I stayed in the bedroom room as it all erupted downstairs "that's it ive done it, I messed up once again." I thought.

After minutes which felt like hours Ben returned upstairs with a phone and plugged it in the upstairs socket. He came into my bedroom and said social services are on the phone if you want to talk to them. I went into the hallway where the phone was plugged in. I spoke to my social worker who asked what was going on. I explained I needed to leave right then. They arranged to pick me up and I was transferred to a children's home in Yeovil. This case was left unresolved.

I moved from children home to children home I felt unloved and not wanted.

I started to self harm by cutting my arms and overdosing. At first they were just small cuts. I realized this was a release. I felt I deserved the pain these caused and it help me to clear all the anger and hatred I had inside. Over time my self harming became more severe and out of control. Care homes were struggling to keep me and I was transferred to several behavioral units. I had, had enough; my anger grew with both myself and the world. I suffered flashbacks as a result of my abuse in the past.

I was still only just 14 but I saw no future. It was just a long red line for me. My anger erupted. I attacked people. I wouldn't talk incase of fear of being rejected. I was classed and labeled out of control. They only saw the behavioral side of it. But what they didn't realize was my whole mind was out of control, my whole life was out of control.

CHAPTER SIX

I was in a private behavioral unit when I received a phone call off my sister Sarah. "Go pack your bags your coming home".

I knew I wouldn't be able to go home because I had a full care order imposed upon me by social services and the courts. But I done as I was asked and Sarah arranged to meet me at my care home.

I was 2-1 staffed. [Which meant I had 2 staff with me at all times] but I asked for some privacy so I could speak to my sister.

As I went into the kitchen to speak with Sarah she told me to leave my bags and when she leaves to see her off to the car. I had to tell the care staff I was just going to see my sister off then when she opened the door I had to jump in.

I done this and I was free.

I hadn't got the exact reasons why this was going on but I had such an adrenalin rush I didn't care. We drove around motorway services so we could avoid home as that would be the first place the police would go. We drove round for a few hours as my sister kept close contact with my mother so we knew when it would be safe to go home.

When we were given the all clear and arrived home. I wanted to find out what was going on. Mum just mentioned that she wasn't sure what but something suspicious was going on between the care home and doctors and she sensed it's not good so arranged to come and collect me.

I went and had a bath and put myself to bed it had been a long day. Little did I realize this was just the start?

It was early hours of the morning when I heard a bang on our front door. Then came a load of shouting and feet were scattering everywhere. My sister Sarah ran up to my room and told me to shut my door and block the door with cupboards and wardrobes. I done as I was instructed to do.

Then I heard my sister yelling in pain. I pulled all the wardrobes away from the door to see what was going on. I could see my sister Sarah getting restrained and hand cuffed by the police whilst other members of the family were being arrested and taken into a riot van. The police recognized me and took me away with them.

I later found out that my sister and her partner were arrested for abduction and dangerous driving.

At this point I was assessed by a psycaritrist and taken into a psychiatric hospital on section which was a private hospital and out of county.

I was detained under the mental health act for a further 7 and half years. From the age of 14-21.

CHAPTER SEVEN

I was in St Andrews Northampton private hospital for 3 and a half years until I was 18.

During my time there I was heavily medicated and at the age of 15 on more than 50 tablets a day.

I was first diagnosed with post traumatic stress disorder and over the years was diagnosed with several other mental health problems until the age of 18 which I was eventually diagnosed with emotionally unstable personality disorder.

At 15 I was told I was beyond help and would never recover.

My self harm detereated and became more serious and life threatening. It got to the point where no hospitals would take my referrals due to them not being able to keep me safe from myself.

I became a very angry person with life and the world in general. I hated being alive I had nothing or no one. And all I wanted was to give up and die. Everyone else had given up on me and I wanted to give up on myself.

I was drugged up until I couldn't move out of bed to get changed or go to the toilet, until I couldn't speak as my speech was so slurred, until I was no longer a human being. I was out of sight and out of mind. Just left to rot. Well that's how it felt.

I became a very angry violent person. I hated myself and the world. And I didn't care who I hurt along the way. I had nothing to loose. But now I sit and realize. I lost a lot during that time. I lost my dignity and self respect. I lost my confidence and my self esteem. I lost my own logic to life. I became violent and unpredictable.

I couldn't hold down any form of relationships whether this is friends, family, or professional.

I couldn't handle anyone getting close for fear that I may be hurt or rejected.

My family had given up on me they got on with their own lives and I wasn't part of that. They were all very close to each other and my family started to feel like strangers to me.

CHAPTER EIGHT

When I was transferred back to a local secure unit where I continued to stay for a further 3 years. Slowly my life felt like it was starting to come together.

I met my present partner Luke. He was a married man but his marriage had come to an end a long time before we were in a relationship.

He had 3 previous children and suffered with obsession compulsive disorder [ocd] and depression.

His OCD was very extreme and effected his day to day living hence the reason Luke was in hospital.

After Luke had left hospital and moved into a place of his own our relationship continued. I had leave granted from hospital and used this to go and visit Luke. [Luke also came regularly to visit me in hospital.]

I fell pregnant whilst in hospital with Luke's baby. I miscarried at 6 weeks.

Very quickly after my miscarriage I became pregnant for a second time.

As I was still in hospital my doctor had to inform social services. Who jumped on my back straight away and started to do assessments.

When I was about 8 months pregnant I came off my section and went into emergency accommodation in Taunton.

I was discharged from hospital as it was too high a risk to keep me in there whilst I as heavily pregnant due to the amount of violence.

CHAPTER NINE

I moved in to my first ever place I was 21 years old.

I had never experienced any form of independence in my life before. I had just spent many years in care and 7 years in psychiatric care. I found it difficult to adjust to "normal" living. I had gone from one extreme of having my independence taken away to having all my independence. Not only this but I was expecting my first child in 4 weeks time.

I found it hard to adjust to even the basics of living. I was very institualised. I found it frightening and used to get so distressed with even simple things like holding a metal knife and fork. I had just spent 7 years with not even having one of these in sight let alone being allowed to use one. To me these seemed so sharp and dangerous after living on flimsy plastic ones for nearly half my life. And as if this wasn't hard enough for me to deal with but my neighbor was throwing me constant abuse and threatening me.

I was so scared that at night I slept with a knife by my bed.

I was very quickly given a 2 bedroom place in my hometown where I grew up as a child. I was aware my family were all still local and thought that this may give us all chance to forgive and forget and make up for lost years.

How wrong was I yet again!

CHAPTER TEN

Social services had been involved since the beginning of my pregnancy due to me falling pregnant in hospital. They had completed assessments on me and asked me to agree to go into a family assessment center after I had the child. They had arranged it so that I would stay in hospital after the birth for 5 days then I would go straight to the private family assessment center which was based in Taunton.

I was in the assessment center for 6 months. It was a very strict assessment. You had cameras in every room and were watched 24hrs a day. They expected you to be perfect. If there was just something small they made a big issue out of it and put you down.

It made me feel hopeless and such a terrible mum. What they don't take into consideration is every first time mum needs to learn. There's no written book on how to be a mother all you can do is try your best and learn from each experience. But being here you were not allowed to learn, it had to be perfect. If it wasn't to any particular member of staffs liking. [This changed daily depending what staff was working] Which each had there own book of rules of how to be a perfect mum, then in there eyes you have failed as a mum. I personally still ask the question. Is there such thing as a perfect mum?

Some days the intensity just became too much for me and on one occasion I resulted in self harming.

I didn't do this in front of my son. I would never even dream of that. I cut my arm but it didn't need treatment. But within an hour of this incident it gave the perfect opportunity for social services to take me to court, to try and get an emergency care order to take my son of me.

I still believe until this day that social services were going to take my baby off me no matter what I done. I believe they decided this before my baby was even born. They just had to get a good enough case before they took action. But even when they tried to get this emergency care order. Their application failed because I had not put my baby at any risk.

The moment I gave birth to my son Jack in February 2009 my life changed I knew I had a responsibility and that now there was no turning back. Jack was beautiful. I knew as I held Jack that this baby would always remain very special to me.

CHAPTER ELEVEN

As court proceedings went on. Social services were looking at Jack being adopted due to my past and my mental health history.

I loved Jack with all my heart yet social services stood in the court room and said to the judge they had no doubt of the mothers [that was me] love for the child. But yet they could still stand and say that because I cut myself I would cut my child, because of my mothers violence to me as a child I would treat my child the same. They even tried to say that because of my history of sexual abuse that there was a risk I would do the same. How they could think this sickens me if anything I would make sure this never happened to my child and do my best to protect him. The judge knew this and wouldn't accept this. In the end Jack was removed from me INCASE of neglect due to my mental illness.

I recall very clearly this moment. I broke down and fell to my knees. The pain was indescribable. I was removed from the court room with my barrister because I was so distressed and everyone was trying to come over and talk to me to comfort me. But no words were going to be able to comfort me or ease this overwhelming pain. My heart was literally torn to pieces.

I remember coming out of the court room and shortly after my sister followed. She was in tears aswel. It was a difficult moment and defiantly not one to find the right words. My sister just said "thank you" and I just said "look after him and let him know how much I love him and I always will."

I was very fortunate in that my elder sister came forward to take Jack on under special guardianship to avoid adoption. She felt that way Jack would stay in the family and know his birth family.

My sister had to various assessments by social services. She had to have her own children's medical records looked at. Answer questions which she felt under pressure to answer correctly and have two people state in her favor that she was a good mother to take Jack on and that he would be well looked after.

I was granted regular contact by the court and I was also told that if my current circumstances change then there could be a possibility of having Jack back.

Eventually Jack went to live with my sister just before his first Christmas. It was a gradual move to make sure that he was settling into the family ok and that her children accepted the change in their life's aswel.

This was a very painful situation to have my own flesh and blood removed from my care. To know he would grow up and call my sister mummy. To know it would be my sister who saw his first step, heard his first words. I loved and still love Jack with all my heart yet he was whipped away from me because of my illness. It hurt right in my sole. I felt to blame. Why did my precious baby have to be taken away because of something that wasn't my fault? My heart was torn and broken.

CHAPTER TWELVE

Over time I came across George and Sally who came from the local Christian center.

I was a mess when I met them. Wrapped up in hurt, pain and anger. I was torn inside out. I spoke with George and Sally about losing Jack and as I got to know them I spoke a bit about my past.

George and Sally told me about the lord, how he understood how I was feeling and could find me the peace I was in desperate need off. I didn't believe this at first I thought how can anything or anyone could repair my broken heart and my destroyed mind. It was all so torn and messed up. But I soon learnt over time god isn't just anything or anyone. He became my savior, my comfort, my councilor and not one thing was out of his control or of his capabilities.

I joined one of the churches coffee mornings and I became to know George and Sally very well along with many others at the church.

Over time I handed over my life to Jesus. Dramatically my whole life changed I started to feel happy, started to feel at peace, gained my confidence and my self esteem. Came to love myself and the lord and slowly I learnt to trust the lord. It wasn't easy; at the start the changes scared me. I started to love life enjoy my life and wonder how I ever considered ending my life. Life was beautiful. Never easy but beautiful.

These changes scared me. Not only me but also worried doctors as I seemed happy. They even considered sectioning me again at one point because I seemed to have picked up too quick. They said it was unexplainable to have such a dramatic change and thought that I was relapsing, as so many times before I went high and came down with a bang and this was there explanation about why I seemed to be happy and loving life in such a short amount of time.

I tested god just like I did all the others. The enemy had a perfect hold over me because of my past. He pushed me off track on more than one occasion he really set out to destroy my relationship with god and my new found life.

I was blessed upon blessed by the lord and I really couldn't understand at first why someone my lord wanted so much good for me. I sinned upon sinned as the devil took hold of me.

Then on one occasion the devil took hold of me good and well.

CHAPTER THIRTEEN

I went back to see one of my abusers John. But I took a knife. I wasn't going to hurt the man. I just wanted answers about what happened when I was a child. I took the knife for my own protection.

I was 23 at the time of this happening. It was just before Christmas 2009. In fact the 12th December 2009. On my way to Johns I knew I was doing wrong and that this could end dangerously. I made a phone call to the crisis team who worked for the mental health out of hours. My heart was pounding with fear but my body ran on overdrive on the adrenalin. My mind said Come on your half way to finding out the truth having all your questions answered. If you don't do it now it will never do it. After I made my phone call to the mental health out of hours. I traveled on up to the address John lived at when the abuse happened. I just prayed that it was still where he was living.

As I approached the address flashbacks from my abuse I had suffered there overtook my mind.

I was drowned with fear so I moved back to the top of the road and sat on the wall so that I could try and compose myself. As I sat on the wall. 4 police cars approached me. Police officers got out of all 4 vehicles and started to walk towards me. They asked me my name, and what I was doing sat on the wall. My head was flooding with all sorts of feelings and fears. My body just went numb as it tried to control my feelings. The police officers took my bag off me which contained the knife with other household items. In the background I could hear an officer saying to me "we are arresting you on possession of a bladed weapon in a public place without lawful reason." As I heard these words. My arms were taken and I was doubled handcuffed and put into the police vehicle. I became hysterical. Shouting and screaming as I was taken to the local police station and chucked into a police cell. As I sat in the police cell my weeping echoed around the big cold room.

I was alone, I was crying but no one heard my cry. What have I done?

CHAPTER FOURTEEN

Unfortunately I was arrested on a Saturday and I had been held in custody all weekend until the Monday when I was due to appear before the court.

During the weekend in the cells I was constantly trying to harm myself in hope of killing myself. This was it my life was over.

I went to the magistrate's court on the Monday. I was remanded to prison for my own safety. As I was told my whole mind was a blur. I was going to Eastwood park prison in Glostershire. As I was put into the sweatbox. [This was the security van that moved you to and from prison to court.] As I sat in the sweatbox tears started to roll down my face. I had never experienced so much fear in my life then I did at this moment in time. Inside my body and my throat was a huge lump as reality hit me. I wasn't going home to my partner, to my freedom. I was the low of the lowest, going to prison with murderers and rapists. How could this be happening am I in reality? I'm no murderer, I'm no rapist. As thoughts welled through my frightened mind. I approached big gates with a large fence around it and barbed wire. This was it I'm here.

The van was checked for drugs at reception then someone from the reception desk got onto the van and tapped my door. "Name please?"

Emily Collins I replied. I got off the van handcuffed and went into reception.

I was bombarded with question after question. "How are you feeling" [how do they think I felt. Excited. I don't think so.] Do you take drugs?' do you sell yourself? Are you pregnant? [What kind of person do you really think I am?] And as if this wasn't intimidating enough I was put through a complete strip search, I was asked to lift up my breasts and open my bottom crack. I have never felt so humiliated.

I was then sent into to see a nurse, then a doctor who asked me to do a urine test. I had enough of all this humiliation and refused. So I was sent to a detox wing full of addicts.

I was chucked into a cell with just my night stuff and an envelope. I opened the envelope and inside was 2 pictures which I carried in my purse. One of my son, and one of my partner. As I looked at these photos my whole world fell apart. Will I ever see these people again? I completely broke down.

I looked around the cell there was graffiti all over the walls sanitary towels stuck to the walls. Dirt all over the floor, and a wooden bed. Stained pillow to lay my head on along with a thin duvet which had far passed its best of days.

I could here other prisoners shouting 'hey girl, hey girl, what's your name, don't cry it's not that bad" I sat and thought if this isn't bad then where the hell have they been. I've never been subjected to anything so vile and disgusting. I would rather die. And this was the start to my 7 months of prison life.

The system was in no hurry of dealing with my case. I was waiting upon report after report from doctors, psycharitrists, probation ect. Court dates were continuously cancelled. And my patience was running thin. It didn't matter what you said or how you acted it just never speeded the process up. I felt so hopeless; I felt this would go on forever.

Being on remand I found particularly hard to cope with as it meant you didn't know what was happening one day to the next. You couldn't get into education as you didn't know if you were going home soon or not. It meant you were limited with what courses you could take on as you didn't know if you would have time to complete them before you maybe went home or were transferred to another prison. I did manage to do a few of the shorter courses and came home with a few qualifications. I was very proud of these qualifications as due to my chaotic childhood my schooling was disrupted and I never managed to sit any exams. In one sense these qualifications were proof to myself that I wasn't stupid or hopeless and gave me the confidence and encouragement to want to further my qualifications in the future.

You only found that out 9pm the night before you were due to shipped on. [Moved to another prison.] So you were always held in anxiety.

At least if you had your sentence you knew there was an end to this terrible nightmare and you could have some hope.

You need to bear in mind one day in prison is like a year on the out. [Apart from at least if your in the community you can go shopping, swimming, gym, bowling] whatever you fancied you have your freedom. Me I was locked up in a stinking dirty cell. With no hope of when I was returning home. When I would next see my partner or my son. Or even if I ever would. I really wasn't coping. I managed to get myself in some kind of routine. A typical prison day would include the following.

8am-9am—tidy cell, mop floor, breakfast, medication, and special meds. [I learnt was methadone]

9am-11am-education or work

11am-12pm—cell count. Behind your door. [People count, in your cell]

12pm-12.30pm—lunch

12.30pm-2pm-in your cell. Post delivered to your cell.

2pm-5pm-education or work

5pm-6pm-in your cell, cell count

6pm-6.30pm-tea

6.30pm-7pm-in your cell, cell count

7pm-8pm-associaton [mixing] in your cell for the night. [Upstairs and down stairs alternate nights]

8pm-8am-in your cell.

8am—back to stage one of a new day

At times of coping I managed a typical prison day. But the majority of the times I was not coping and my self harm deteriated severely.

Then it became more than self harm I wanted out and I don't mean prison, I mean my life.

I couldn't face another day. I started ligaturing they became tighter and tighter until each time I needed oxygen to keep me alive. Then one day it went too far.

I lay on my bed for several days. I couldn't get comfortable as through anxiety my body was fitting when I relaxed and when I stood I was collapsing. My mind was far from at rest and I had had enough. I felt as if my body was just going to shut down and die. I felt that my body could not handle the state I was in and that I was dying. I lay in my cell on the bed just waiting and praying for my heart to stop. The beating got slower and slower. My body was unable to move or respond. My sight had gone. I felt dead but I could still hear my heart. I lay on my cell bed pleading for all this to stop.

The prison staff had got a psycaritrist to come and see me. They thought I had completely gone insane through stress and I was even questioning it myself. I knew how I felt was scary and frightening and I had never experienced this before in my life. The pshcaritrist prescribed some antipsychotics and anti anxiety tablets.

As he left the cell I forced myself to move. I grabbed a ligature and tied it around my neck. I lay there patiently waiting to die. My head began becoming light; my thoughts were slowly fading and quieting down. My mind started to feel peaceful as I headed towards the light I could see in the distance.

When I came around I had tubes down my throat and was having heart compressions. A room of 15 people crying. 2 ambulance men and a governor, speaking, ready to confirm my death. I realized I had just died. But someone saved my life. It wasn't just anyone who saved me. It was God, he had a plan for me and he wasn't letting me go until I fulfilled his plan.

I felt a mixture of emotions. I felt anger because I was brought back to this horrible place in my mind when I was so peaceful. But then I felt joy because one day I could watch my baby boy playing and smiling and return home to my dear Luke. This day was the start of a new life for me. I had been given a second chance.

Even though prison staff and the nurses were convinced I would not come out of prison alive. I did as that's why I can sit here today and be given the chance to tell my story. A lot of people accidentally end up killing themselves through self harm. I did not let this beat me. I was one of the very lucky few to be given a second chance. And I knew this. I knew that something big had to happen so I didn't let self harm finish me off and end up killing me.

From then on during my times of severe distress I was placed on a vulnerable wing for my own safety. I later learnt this was known and referred to as the ponses wing. I learnt this after realizing this wing was also where they placed high profile cases for there own safety. One of the high profile cases who were on this wing was a child abuser which was why this wing was known to the other girls as the ponses wing. During my times on these wings. I came face to face with this pedophile daily. She was the cleaner for this wing and done my washing. I was also faced with another high profile case lady who starved her 2 children to death and also another who overdosed a lady in a nursing home. To ever think I was near any of these people brings a real sickness feeling to my throat.

This was when I sat and thought where is my life really going? What do I really want? This not only made me look at life this way but it made me appreciate all the things that I had once taken for granted. Just things like walking down the town, popping to the shop, seeing and speaking to my friends, having a hug or a talking to my partner, watching a film and even accepting any help that was offered. Nearly loosing my life, my freedom had really made me realize just how important these are to me and I was determined to never let anything or anyone in my life take me to this point again.

It wasn't easy I had to work hard especially seems I was so addicted to self harm. But just like any other addiction I had to find other ways of coping. I had to find a replacement. But a safer replacement and if things got really bad all I had to do was remember the dark place I went to.

For years people used to say to me sometimes you have to hit the lowest to rise up again. I used to think how many times have I got to hit the lowest so this could happen. But I tell you I only ever realized what the lowest was when it didn't just become mental but physical as well. To the point where I was in so much anxiety I was fitting when I slept or when I relaxed and my heart started to slow down, and when I stood I was collapsing no matter how much I ate or drank. But to confirm I was at my lowest. I was in prison. The low of the lowest. You couldn't get any lower than the degrading, humiliating and embarrassment of being in prison in a place so disgusting with some high profile dangerous people.

To cope with self harm urges I had to find some distraction techniques. It was surprising how many hobbies I realized I had when using my distraction techniques. When I felt low, and didn't feel I was coping very good I started to do some cross stitching, latch hook rug making, painting, poetry, reading, gym, swimming ect. I used to do as many things as I could and I tell you these were all far more beneficial than adding to any of my scars or risking my whole life.

Thinking this way helped me deal with prison in a different manor. I had done all the rebelling and being charged and put in front of the governor. I had done all the having to go without my canteen sheet. [This was where you had a list so you could buy from the shop]. I had done all the going without association. [Times out your cell] I even plenty of times had to stay behind my door 24hrs a day as a punishment.

I rebelled many times. My anger got the better of me many times and I let it explode. I took my anger out on the other prisoners. [Not the best way to go] and to the staff. Who I physically attacked and was regularly restrained.

[That wasn't the best way either because during one restraint a member of staff broke her wrist and I was charged with ABH. [Actual bodily harm]. And that charge was still pending when I returned to the community.

The best release I did find with dealing with my anger was using the prison gym. It was far more constructive and didn't get me into more trouble and dig me further into a whole. I used the gym daily. You had one opportunity to use the gym at 8am-9am. But it meant missing breakfast. Which I was happy to do as I knew I would not miss my two bits of toast which were more like bread they were so undercooked.

Visits and letters meant the world to me. My partner wrote to me regularly that helped to keep me going. It kept me in some connection with the outside world. George, Sally and Luke also came to visit me on a couple of occasions. And George, Sally and Luke also used to attend all my court hearings which were a great support. They really did do there best to keep me going and to try and help me not to look at things so negatively.

It was coming up to my sentencing date. I was coping a lot better in prison than I was. I was just trying to make the best out of a bad situation. I knew if I could get to the point I was managing in prison. I was sure whatever came across me when I regained my freedom I could defiantly face. I knew I would never manage to cope in prison alone. And one day I sat thought how can I do this alone. I have no one in here. Then suddenly god spoke to me. He said I did not have to be alone, only if I choose to and that he was there. With hearing this message I leaned on God. I prayed every night and every morning. I prayed for peace, strength and the courage to carry on. I went to the prison chapel every Sunday. It was only at this time that I realized there really was a God. I found that when I was consistent with my prayer and talking to God. God was consistent with me and my days became more manageable and I never felt alone. But when I pulled back and took a back seat from god. Then so did God which resulted in my days becoming unmanageable again until eventually I turned back to God through prayer. God really showed his light to me, his peace and his love and I knew from this day on where in life I went wrong.

CHAPTER FIFTEEN

It was the court hearing before the final hearing and things were not looking good. No reports were complete that the court had requested and my bail application had failed.

As I was in the police cell waiting to go up into court I sat and prayed with God. I asked God to speak through the judge's mouth so that I knew it was God's choice what happened to me from there and no individuals. It was a big request from me for God and I underestimated God and thought it was unlikely that could happen. As I was hand cuffed and taken up the steps to the courtroom I sat down with all hope gone.

The judge fumed that court time had been wasted as we were only asking for adjournment and written responses were ordered from my solicitor firm and the doctor who we were waiting to do the report on me.

As the judges anger raised so did my anxiety as I realized I defiantly was making that 2 hour journey back to the nightmare of prison life.

The judge ordered "Emily may you please rise." I stood legs shaking as I prepared myself for the judges anger to erupt on me. But in a calm voice the judge said. "I am very sorry we have had a hearing like this. I have no choice but to remand you for a further 2 weeks. But let me assure you there will not be another hearing like this."

Thoughts span through my mind. My partner was in the court room, he so much wanted me to go home. I could feel his anger from where I was sat. He's going to think this is my fault. As these thoughts span through my mind the judge continued. "This is not your fault and im sorry this has happened, its unacceptable but let me also assure you this case will be dealt with quickly. Take her down."

As I went back to prison I lay in my cell. Thinking "back here yet again." As the day rolled through my head. I suddenly realized what the judge had said. He said "Emily." A judge NEVER calls you by your first name. It's either Miss Collins or the defendant.

I then looked further into what the judge had said. "This is not your fault. This case will be dealt with quickly. It's unacceptable." As the judge spoke it was as if he knew what I was thinking. Then I realized that wasn't the judge speaking to me. It was God speaking through the judge's mouth. God had answered my prayer. I cried in amazement but also with how ashamed I felt. I underestimated god and I learnt never to underestimate God again and my faith and trust grew in god to a deeper level. I studied the bible and tears flowed as I read the passage. God calls you by name. That it was he done in my hearing called me by name.

As my next case continued, 2 weeks later it was my sentencing date. Whatever was going to happen would happen this day as progress had been made and all reports were finished?

I once again took the 2 hour journey down to court. As I sat in the van watching the fields go by. I thought in a few hours I will be making this journey back again. I had convinced myself I was going back to prison and that I was looking at least 2 years. I still had at least 15 months to serve. How I would manage I hadn't worked that out as of yet.

I had prayed to the Lord that he would find me mercy. I knew I shouldn't have committed that crime and I was truly sorry. I had continually spoken to God through my time in prison coming towards the end. I had developed a good relationship with God. I asked the Lord to do what he felt was right during my final hearing. If it was right for me to go back to prison, then send me back but if it was right for me to return home then send me home.

I had learnt by now I needed God in my life and now I was willing to commit myself to the Lord. I prayed for mercy and repented my sins.

As I was called into court my legs were like jelly. In my head I was asking God to be with me and take control.

I stood before the judge then I was sent back to the cells as the judge needed time to read the reports.

As I sat in the cell tears streamed down my face. My future was in front of me but I didn't know what it was going to be.

In the police cell I fell to my knees in distress as I asked the Lord please give me another chance. But still if I need to go back to prison then send me back.

I was called back into the court room. The judge heard the case then asked me to rise. I could barley stand with anxiety of what was going to happen. As my mind said this is it. The judge responded Miss Collins. You obviously have a lot of problems that need resolving. I do not condemn your actions but to me it is very clear you need help overcoming these problems. It is for this reason I grant you a community order to work with the mental health team and a supervision order to make sure you receive the support. I do not want to see you back in this court again. You are free to leave. With this I nearly fell to the floor my mind couldn't take it. I was going home. Thank you Lord, thank you so much. This was the start to my blessings with my Savior.

I can see during my time in prison when I walked away from the lord things became very difficult but when I let the Lord in my times were more bearable. I believe this was one thing that showed me who the Lord was and what my life could be. It made me see the Lord in a complete new light and I just wanted to keep growing in the Lord's love.

CHAPTER SIXTEEN

After leaving prison I returned to my home with my partner. I came home as a complete different girl. My whole attitude to life had changed. I loved life and for once I was ready to live life to the full and take all life opportunities that came to me on. No-one recognized me when I came home. I had lost a lot of weight, I had matured and people commented how different my voice even sounded. Even my mental health team who had known me for 3 years didn't recognize me or couldn't even believe the difference in me.

When I went away I was a desperate girl who saw no future or even cared for a future and when I came back I loved nothing more than life and to live for the next day the next year the next decade. I didn't want my life to end. To me my life had only just started. I felt content. That does not mean there wasn't times I struggled or had a bad day. But my bad days were human it didn't mean I wanted to die.

For some people when they go to prison it makes them worse and they end up in and out of prison for most there life's. This definitely wasn't me. Prison was the worst thing and scariest thing I had gone through but it made me have plenty of thinking time to realize I needed to let go of all my hurt, anger and pain and to me this was just the beginning.

My whole life changed around my relationship with my partner. He had moved on so far since my time in prison but for the better. Our relationship was a lot stronger and we never took each other for granted. We learnt to honor every minute we had together.

My partner's ocd had moved on along way. It was like coming home to a complete different man. I think because I was away in prison for 7 months my partner had to vend for himself. But in one sense it was a good thing as it meant he had to learn new ways of coping and overcoming the problems he had with his daily living due to his illness of ocd.

CHAPTER SEVENTEEN

When I first came home there was one thing causing me a lot of anxiety and preventing me at first moving on with my life. Whilst I was in prison at one point when I was restrained an officer injured there wrist and I was charged with actual bodily harm. This meant when I was released I had still had this charge pending. I was warned that I was looking at serious time for this charge and each day that went by I prayed that I would not be sent back to prison it was a very slim chance that this didn't happen but praise god as when I went to court I was given compensation rather than prison. The lord really did bless me this day and I knew from this day the Lord was defiantly the way for me.

I had been given another chance and I was going to use this to the full of my ability. From this day on I followed the Lord with each day I had in hand.

CHAPTER
EIGHTEEN

As time went on following my release, the next few months were very moving. I felt over these months I was given a lot of opportunities and that my life really had only just started. Not only did I not end up back in prison. But I received certificates in the post from courses I had done whilst I was in prison. Up until then I had no qualifications at all due to my disrupted childhood. I also received a copy of the women in prison magazine [which women prisons get copies of] with an article published that I wrote on self harm along with a letter I had off the editor to say how girls had already wrote in to say they had found it very helpful.

I also saw in there an opportunity to write the start of my life story to a well known author named Cathy Glass. And I got a very encouraging response which prompted me to write this book.

One thing I haven't mentioned was just before I found the Lord I was looking into a spiritualist church. As I was told by mediums I was in danger if I didn't exercise my so called gifts. But that was a point I felt I needed to make so you can see the Lord saved me just before I faced death. The Lords timing is perfect.

In regards to what happened between me and my family. I no longer have any contact. It was never positive what I had with them. Regardless how many times I tried to make things work. My mother still drinks although she has times where she does very well. My father just cut me off with no explanation.

It was not easy to have to come to a decision that I needed to move on. But I had to forgive to move on. Especially seems I am still very local to them. I live in the same town as them and my mother and sister both only live a couple streets away.

I don't know what the future holds for what's ever going to happen with my family. But at the moment I feel I can move on without them. They were never there for me as a child. They see me as a burden and can't accept me for who I am or what ive been through. In my view I have everything I need in God. And the Lord is better than what any of my family could offer. For God loves me unconditionally. Accepts me for who I am. Knows everything about me and still accepts me and never rejects me.

My walk with the Lord continues. And I continue to find courage and strength in the Lord. At times I stumble but the Lord always gets me back on the right track and even though I sometimes walk away from the Lord. The lord keeps his promise and never walks away from me.

I have met many other Christians through our local church. Whom I love dearly. We pray for each other and keep each other walking on the right path with God.

The best part is my Christian brothers and sisters accept me for who I am. And their love and support means so much to me. Their very positive for me and my future and I continue to walk in my faith with them.

Over time I have formed a much closer relationship with the Lord who I thirst for so bad. I have managed to trust the Lord and allow the Lord to have my baggage which the lord has taken my burden and released me.

To be free of my baggage. To be free to walk with the Lord. To no longer feel trapped in my life and to allow someone to have their way with my life and to guide me was a very challenging move for me and still is at times. But no-one can do for me what the Lord can do. He loves me unconditionally he does not fail me and he keeps his every promise. How awesome.

He's brought me to be able to forgive and to forgive myself. Without the Lord I would have found that impossible. But my strength is the Lord. My strength comes from my heavenly father. Thanks for the blood of Jesus Christ. He was waiting for me for so many years yet he continued to wait and he was ready to take me on with open arms. Most people would have run away from me. My burden was too much. The Lord just stood with his arms open ready to take it from me. I can do nothing but give praise and worship to my God, my councilor my father, my Savior, my king, my life, my everything.

I belong to my father I am a child of God and my father saved me physically and spiritually and I live everyday for him.

I view life as precious now. It's been renewed and transformed. I praise and glorify the Lord for he is my precious gift. I didn't just receive life spiritually but physically aswel. He brought me back from death spiritually and physically. I am on this earth for a reason just like each one of us is. The father has had his hand on me from the very start. At my times of trouble my father was there but I just hadn't seeked him. Praise God for he knows all my failures and troubles but yet has forgiven me because of the blood of Christ. I live for my father; I yearn for my father I seek in my father at all times. My life I give to my father so he can use me in whatever way he wants for his will is always good. My journey with the lord has been very challenging but I have been blessed through every part of it. I praise God for what I have, for who I am and for all his done. My suffering was nothing compared to how the Lord suffered so that I can be saved. And the Lord has done that for you too.

My life now excites me. Where the Lord is taking me. I'm going to far and high places and it excites me. The plans of the Lord are perfect and how he has worked my life is perfect. I can use all the weaknesses and all the pain I once suffered to strengthen me and encourage me. It encourages me as each day I look at who I was before I was transformed and all I can do is dance for the joy at what I have. My tears at what I lost are now laughter at what I have found. Thank you for the blood of Jesus. I can smile. I can live in fulfillment. I can now live in peace.

My life did not begin in the easiest of ways but I can use my experiences to learn and grow from them. I can either be bitter and angry for the rest of my days but I choose to be a witness that no matter how difficult life becomes you can overcome it. My criminal record makes it difficult for me to work closely with vulnerable people so I can't be a witness that way to show no matter how bad things are there is a future. My future is with God. So I chose to sit and write my story so you can see in black and white I no longer live in the darkness but in the light. I was once told by professionals I was beyond help. But I was never beyond help from the Lord. I was underestimated, I was judged, but I am also a living proof of a survivor. And I hope that my story can help others see hope and be survivors. I'm only 25 and my life has just begun. The light has just been switched on and now I no longer walk in darkness but in the light with the Lord. Praise the heavenly father. Nothing is beyond or out of his control. For he is mighty and powerful beyond all measures.

May the Lord bring you into the light and be with you too?

Lightning Source UK Ltd.
Milton Keynes UK
UKOW052232071111

181630UK00001B/240/P